£7.50

BRANCH LINE TO ALLHALLOWS

including Port Victoria and Grain

Vic Mitchell and Keith Smith

Cover picture: A typical branch train starts its 37 minute journey from Allhallows to Gravesend behind class H no. 31512 in March 1960. (Late Derek Cross)

Design – Deborah Goodridge

First published January 1989

ISBN 0 906520 62 2

© Middleton Press, 1988

Typeset by CitySet - Bosham 573270

Published by Middleton Press
      Easebourne Lane
      Midhurst, West Sussex
      GU29 9AZ
      ☎ (073 081) 3169

Printed & bound by Biddles Ltd,
      Guildford and Kings Lynn

CONTENTS

101.	Allhallows-on-Sea
54.	Beluncle Halt
21.	Cliffe
10.	Denton Halt
74.	Grain
69.	Grain Halt
1.	Gravesend
33.	High Halstow Halt
13.	Hoo Junction
57.	Middle Stoke Halt
12.	Milton Range Halt
88.	Port Victoria
41.	Sharnal Street
60.	Stoke Junction Halt
18.	Uralite Halt

ACKNOWLEDGEMENTS

We are very grateful for the assistance received from many of the photographers mentioned in the credits and from R.M. Casserley, R. Chapman, S. Earl, D. Harris, J.R.W. Kirkby, H. Lingwood, D. Oliver, K. Payne, R. Randell, E. Staff, N. Stanyon, G. Trigwell and Prof. H.P. White. Our wives have been of immeasurable help once again.

GEOGRAPHICAL SETTING

The route commences at Gravesend which is on the dip slope of the chalk of the North Downs. After traversing the alluvium of Shorne and Higham Marshes, the line rises onto the sands of the Thanet Beds, which form a ridge across the Hoo Peninsula. This rises to over 200ft. above sea level and is orientated south-west to north-east. From the summit, near High Halstow, trains descend onto the level land and marshes which form the eastern end of the peninsula and the Isle of Grain.

The village of Cliffe is situated on an outcrop of Chalk, which was for many years of economic importance for cement manufacture. Having low agricultural value, Grain Marsh has been used for armament testing and later for oil refining and other industrial purposes. These commercial activities have resulted from the presence of the exceptionally deep water in the River Medway, near the Isle of Grain.

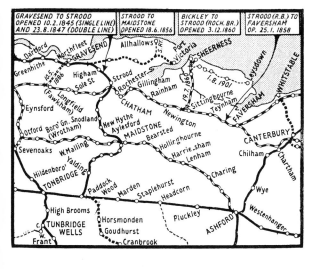

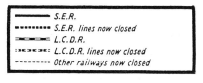

(Railway Magazine)

All maps in this album are to the scale of 25″ to 1 mile, unless otherwise stated.

HISTORICAL BACKGROUND

The South Eastern Railway's line between Gravesend and Strood came into use on 10th February 1845 but, despite a proposal in 1864, a branch to the Hundred of Hoo did not receive parliamentary consent until 21st July 1879. The Hundred of Hoo Railway purchased the necessary land at agricultural prices and was itself acquired by the SER in August 1881.

The line was opened as far as Sharnal Street on 4th April 1882 and services were extended to Port Victoria on 11th September 1882. While the branch did serve the local community, its main purpose was the passage of boat trains in connection with the SER's new steamer service to Flushing for passengers to Belgium. This had been introduced to compete with the London Chatham & Dover Railway's European services from Queenborough Pier at Sheerness, on the opposite shore of the Medway.

In 1899, the SER and the LCDR ceased to be rivals and were managed by a committee as the South Eastern & Chatham Railway. Also in 1899, the Royal Corinthian Yacht Club established its headquarters at Port Victoria and thus some revenue was obtained from wealthy Londoners travelling to their large yachts. This traffic ceased with the advent of World War I, when their premises were taken over by the Royal Naval Air Service.

Continental traffic on the branch was reduced in the years following the formation of the SECR. In an attempt to generate more local traffic, six halts were opened in 1906 and steam railmotors were introduced. These were phased out after only two years, mainly due to their inability to handle peak traffic. Mineral traffic started to grow from 1910, when a cement works was established near Cliffe.

WWI brought an increase in traffic as army and naval depots were established in the area, along with munition works and an airship station. Many extra trains were required for materials and workers. After the war, chemicals and oil products were added to the list of commodities carried from premises on the Medway waterfront.

In 1923, the line became part of the Southern Railway which, in the 1930s, attempted to increase holiday traffic on its lines. A branch was opened to the north coast at Allhallows on 16th May 1932, in the hope that a coastal resort would develop. Despite the bankruptcy of the estate developers, this branch was doubled in 1934 and some traffic in day trippers was carried.

WWII brought an increase in freight business, following an expansion of military depots in the district. In the early 1950s, a massive oil refinery was built on the Isle of Grain, which generated a great increase in rail traffic. On 3rd September 1951, Port Victoria station was closed and a new terminus, known as Grain, was opened, one mile to the west.

Passenger traffic dwindled and services were withdrawn on 4th December 1961, when the extension to Allhallows was closed completely. The refinery continued to make good use of the railway until the early 1980s, when processing ceased and the site became a distribution depot for oil products brought in by sea for partial transport by rail. In recent years, traffic has increased in aggregates, as this material is landed at two locations, originating from the local seabed and from Scotland. Further demand on the single line branch is being made as the number of trains increase in connection with the transport of aggregates and concrete lining segments from the Isle of Grain manufacturing plant to the Channel Tunnels.

Few railways can show so many peaks and troughs in their traffic graphs as this unusual Kent byway. In the mid-1970s, local councils called for the restoration of passenger services and more recently the South Eastern & Chatham Railway Preservation Society was formed to prepare for the acquisition of the branch when it is no longer required by BR. Details of the scheme can be obtained from The Lodge, 16 Berryhill, Eltham Park, London SE9 1QW.

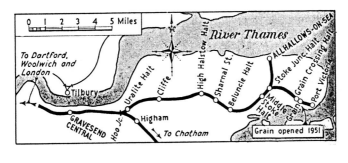

PASSENGER SERVICES

Weekdays

Initially there were six local services daily with two boat trains in connection with the ships to Belgium, and by 1890 there were eight stopping trains. Between 1895 and 1900, the winter service was terminated at Sharnal Street and the ferry service between Port Victoria and Sheerness suspended.

With the formation of the SECR, Port Victoria was theoretically redundant, as shipping could be concentrated on Sheerness (Queenborough). However, following a fire there, the "Flushing Night Mail" returned to Port Victoria until 1904.

The introduction of steam railmotors in 1906 did not increase the number of trains, which remained at about six each way until after the SR was formed. The opening of Allhallows reduced the number of trains to Port Victoria to one at each end of the working day. The new resort however was given 13 trains per day, some of which included through coaches to and from London, but these were withdrawn after only two years. In 1934, there were still 13 trains, three of which ran to and from Gillingham. The summer timetable for 1938 offered one train originating at London Bridge, one at Charing Cross, one at Blackheath, two at Dartford and seven at Gravesend.

Military traffic during WWII resulted in a service of eleven journeys still being shown in 1942 and, in the post war years, a maximum of thirteen were operated each day up to closure. Grain continued to see two workmen's trains, the second one on Saturdays being around noon.

Sundays

In most years up to 1932, three journeys were operated, but sometimes not for the full length of the branch in winter. Summer timetables prior to WWII usually showed 18 trains, several of which started in London or its suburbs. Between 1939 and 1955 there were generally six trips, but thereafter it was increased to thirteen or more in the summer, until 1961 when there were ten. Grain was normally devoid of Sunday trains, except in the summer of 1959 when there was a 1.02 pm departure, with no advertised arrival.

GRAVESEND

1. The terminus of the Gravesend & Rochester Railway was on a site near the river and was opened on 10th February 1845. The line was closed from 13th December 1846 until 23rd August 1847 while Higham and Strood Tunnels were converted from canal and single track to double track. The terminus was closed permanently on 30th July 1849 when a new through station was opened by the SER. This is seen from the down platform, looking towards London. (Lens of Sutton)

The 1897 map shows the location of the turntable and tram tracks in New Road. The cramped layout of the sidings is also evident.

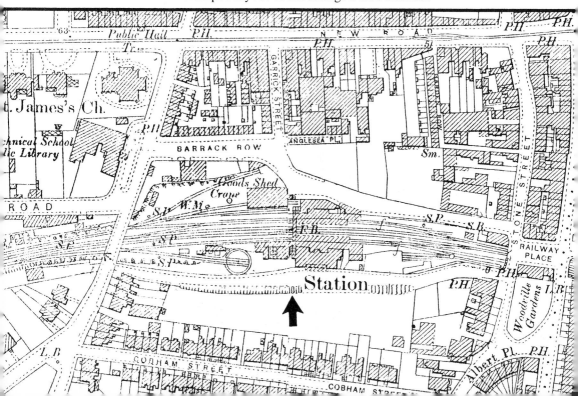

2. The No. 2 signal box is visible in this westward view. The suffix "Central" was added on 1st July 1899 to distinguish it from the former LCDR station which became "West Street" until 1949, and "West" until closure to passengers in 1953. "Central" was dropped on 14th June 1965. (P. Rutherford)

3. Electrification from Dartford on 6th July 1930 and to Gillingham on 2nd July 1939 made the turntable redundant. This bay platform was built in its place and is seen accommodating class R1 no. 1663, which had just been shunted after arrival with the 5.05 pm from Port Victoria on 11th September 1947. (J.H. Aston)

4. The ACV lightweight diesel set worked on the Allhallows branch between 13th October and 16th November 1953. It is seen on 24th October, while class E4 0-6-2T no. 32580 stands in the goods yard, which closed on 6th November 1961. The goods headshunt was the only electrified siding. (R.C. Riley)

5. The main entrance is on the up side, remote from the town centre, and was well established before the rival LCDR station opened on 10th May 1886, at the west end of the town. The south facade was photographed in November 1959. (J.J. Smith)

6. Following the failure of the steam railmotors, their bodies were converted and placed on conventional bogies. Two, formed as set no. 481, are being propelled from the down platform towards Allhallows on 11th September 1959 by one of Wainwright's H class tanks. (T. Wright)

7. The through lines could be used by branch trains for layover between journeys or for run-round purposes. Class C 0–6–0 no. 31244 is signalled from the down through line with set no. 716 and an ex-railmotor set. (Lens of Sutton)

8. The 9.50 am from Allhallows arrives on 11th November 1961 and passes the platform extensions, the down one of which was built on the site of the former spur to a cattle dock. Visible are some of the ten bridges that span the line in about half a mile. (E. Wilmshurst)

9. Viewed from the fourth bridge east of the station, class H no. 31518 accelerates towards Allhallows on 7th August 1961. The indistinct up signals were replaced by colour lights, which, from 1971, were controlled from a new panel box at Dartford. (S.C. Nash)

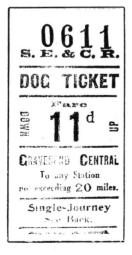

0611

S. E. & C. R.

DOG TICKET

Fare

DOWN 11d UP

GRAVESEND CENTRAL
To any Station
not exceeding 20 miles.

Single-Journey
See Back.

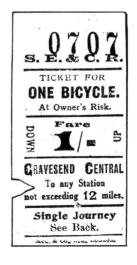

0707

S. E. & C. R.

TICKET FOR
ONE BICYCLE.

At Owner's Risk.

Fare

DOWN 1/- UP

GRAVESEND CENTRAL
To any Station
not exceeding 12 miles.

Single Journey
See Back.

DENTON HALT

10. Opened on 1st July 1906, the halt was served almost exclusively by branch line trains and was therefore closed when the Allhallows service ceased on 4th December 1961. Another 1906 halt was situated at Milton Road, ½ mile east of Gravesend, but this was closed on 1st May 1915. (Lens of Sutton)

11. The gated level crossing was closed on 16th December 1971 and this footbridge, seen in October 1974, was erected on the site of the halt. The conductor rails remained at the centre of the tracks. (D. Cullum)

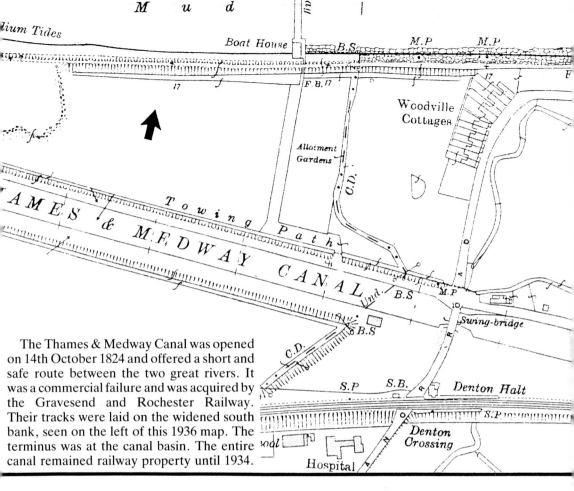

The Thames & Medway Canal was opened on 14th October 1824 and offered a short and safe route between the two great rivers. It was a commercial failure and was acquired by the Gravesend and Rochester Railway. Their tracks were laid on the widened south bank, seen on the left of this 1936 map. The terminus was at the canal basin. The entire canal remained railway property until 1934.

MILTON RANGE HALT

12. Shown in timetables from 1st July 1906 until 17th July 1932, this halt served the nearby rifle ranges. Subsequently it has been used "as required". This photograph of C class no. 31689 on 3rd December 1961 illustrates well the mists which envelope this area of bleak marshland for long periods each winter. For many years a long engineer's siding was provided on the down side, behind the platform. (A.E. Bennett)

HOO JUNCTION

13. The driver of H class 0–4–4T no. 31530 prepares to surrender the single line token on 11th November 1961. The curved eaves were a notable feature of these locomotives. The signal box was taken out of use on 15th May 1971. (E. Wilmshurst)

14. Short platforms were provided on the main line in 1956, for use by railway staff requiring access to this remote location. Electrification of the Kent coast routes started in 1959 and, as part of this scheme, the marshalling yards were fitted with overhead conductors for safety reasons. Unfortunately, a number of firemen had disasters with firing irons touching them. (H.C. Casserley)

15. Looking east from the public foot crossing to Shorne Marshes in 1988, we see the main line rising at 1 in 315 up and the branch junction signal on the left. Empty coal hoppers stand on the right and the TOPS office is to the right of the main line. (V. Mitchell)

Freight train service in July 1937.

UP TRAINS		AM	am	
10.30pm	Queenborough	12.05	12.35	Bricklayers Arms
10.45pm	Paddock Wood	12.55	1.40	Bricklayers Arms
8.10pm	Dover Town	1.50	2.25	Hither Green
6.45pm	Dover Town via Ramsgate	2.40		
			2.45	Gravesend Central
			3.15	Hither Green
			5.00	Hither Green
11.35pm	Redhill	5.05		
			5.22	Northfleet
7.20am	Higham	7.25		
6.17am	Chatham	8.05		
			10.05	Dartford
5.00am	Tonbridge	11.13	pm	
4.00am	Woking via Tonb	11.30	12.25	Angerstein Wharf
10.05am	Port Victoria	11.20		
8.55am	Dover Town	1.20pm	1.53	Hither Green
2.00pm	Port Victoria	4.48	5.57	Greenhithe
2.15pm	Maidstone West	5.10		
5.50pm	Chatham	6.15		
6.33pm	Strood	7.05	9.25	Hither Green
6.50pm	Miskin Siding	7.40		
3.35pm	Paddock Wood	7.40		
6.45pm	Allhallows on S.	8.27		
*3.35pm	Bekesbourne	8.15	9.00	Blackfriars*
*8.25pm	Higham	8.30		

* Market trains run when required.

The marshalling yard at Hoo Junction developed over the years to the point where it became one of the seven major yards in the Eastern Section of the Southern Railway. At its zenith the Down Yard, situated in the fork between the Main line and the Isle of Grain branch, consisted of three 'through' sidings and three dead end sidings with a total capacity of 219 wagons. There was also a triangle for turning locomotives.

The Up Yard was much bigger. The entrance was from the up line before the junction while the exit was on the Gravesend side of the junction. Trains from the Isle of Grain branch had to reverse into the yard which had two reception lines, a departure

DOWN TRAINS.		Arrive am	Depart am	
			2.00	Brighton via Maidstone W/Redhill
12.50am	Dartford	2.25		
12.35am	Angerstein Whf	2.50	3.15	Woking via Maidstone W/Redhill
			3.35	Dover Town via Canterbury East
12.53am	Bricklayers Arms	3.50		
			4.40	Allhallows on Sea
5.05am	Gravesend Central	5.15		
			5.45	Higham
			7.05	Chatham Goods
			7.46	Port Victoria
8.32am	Northfleet	8.47		
			8.50	Paddock Wood
			10.20	Maidstone West
9.00am	Hither Green	10.48	11.50	Port Victoria
11.48am	Dartford	1.03pm	pm	
			3.20	Strood
2.06pm	Dartford	3.28		
			7.16	Hither Green via Maidstone W/Tonbridge
			9.00	Chatham
7.47pm	Greenhithe	9.49	12.10	Newington

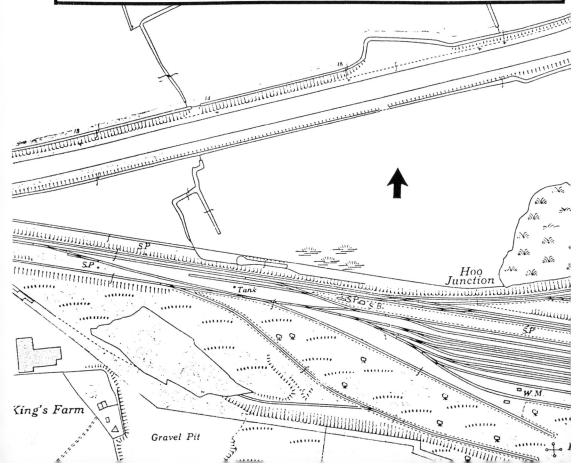

line, 14 dead-end sidings and 2 shunt necks. The total capacity of the Down Yard sidings was 728 wagons.

The Yard's function was to collect wagons from all stations and sidings between Dartford in the east and the Isle of Sheppey in the west including the Isle of Grain Branch and stations to Maidstone West, probably the most industrialised area on the Southern. The yard also fed the same stations with trunk services to and from Hither Green, Bricklayers Arms, Tonbridge and Dover.

Soon after amalgamation, the Southern Railway set about its suburban electrification which necessitated diverting as much freight traffic as possible out of the London area. Hoo Junction played its part in this exercise. From July 1926, a service was introduced each way between Woking and Angerstein Wharf via Redhill, Maidstone West and Hoo Junction. In July 1930, following the concentration of all goods traffic at Redhill on the ex-LBSCR Goods Depot, the old No. 3 yard was converted for marshalling purposes and a new train introduced between Hoo Junction and Brighton, via Redhill. The return train started from Redhill.

This map at 20″ to 1 mile shows the Up Yard as opened on 23rd October 1927.

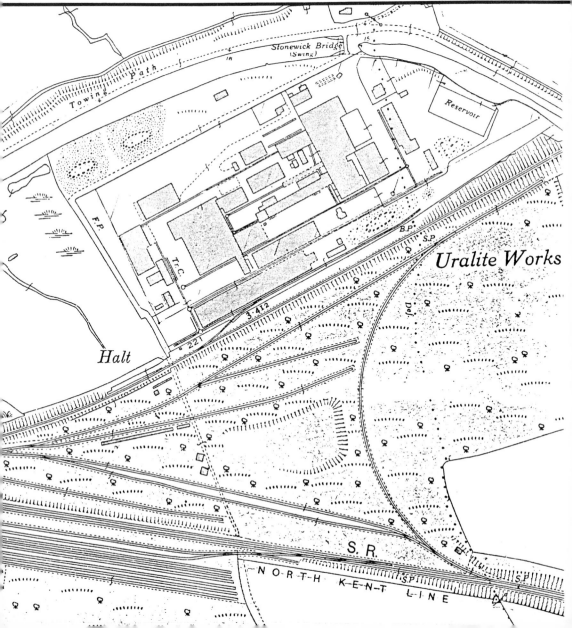

16. The commencement of the branch is viewed from an up train pausing at the Staff Halt on 27th August 1988. In the centre are condemned vans standing in the former ballast sidings and out of the picture, on the left, is Smeath Metals siding, in use until December 1986. (V. Mitchell)

GRAVESEND CENTRAL and PORT VICTORIA.—South Eastern and Chatham.

Miles.		Week Days.																	Sundays.			
		mrn	mrn		aft		aft		aft	aft	aft	aft		aft		aft			mrn	aft	aft	
	Gravesend Central ¶..dep.	7 50	1112	Sats.	2 22	Except Sats.	2 25	Sats.	3 45	5 33	6 37	8 12	Sats.	8 50	Sats.	9 55	....	....	1040	3 8	6 8	....
5¾	Cliffe	8 4	1129		2 34		2 42		3 55	5 43	6 50	8 22		9 2		10 7	....	....	1055	3 23	6 23	....
9½	Sharnal Street ¶	8 12	1137		2 40		2 50		4 6	5 51	6 58	8 28		9 10		1015	....	....	11 3	3 31	6 31	....
15¾	Port Victoria.........arr.	8 31	1152		2 55		3 5		4 25	6 6	7 13	8 42		9 28		....	....	....	1118	3 46	6 46	....

Miles.		Week Days.																Sundays.			
		mrn	mrn	aft	aft		aft	aft		aft	aft		aft					aft	aft	aft	
	Port Victoria ¶........dep.	8 0	9 2	1250	3 55	Sats.	4 35	6 14	Sats.	7 55	9 0	Sats.	....	....	....	....	....	1215	5 10	7 18	....
6¼	Sharnal Street	8 18	9 16	1 4	4 9		4 49	6 28		8 5	9 12		1035	....	....	....	....	1229	5 24	7 32	....
10	Cliffe ¶....[261, 626, 631	8 26	9 25	1 13	4 18		4 58	6 37		8 12	9 19		1041	....	....	....	....	1238	5 33	7 42	....
15¾	Gravesend Central 252 arr.	8 37	9 42	1 29	4 35		5 13	6 52		8 23	9 30		1052	....	....	....	....	1253	5 48	7 57	....

Extra (3rd class only).—Gravesend Central to Uralite Halt at 5 30 mrn., not stopping.

¶ "Halts" at Milton Road, Denton, Milton Range, and Uralite, between Gravesend Central and Cliffe; High Halstow, between Cliffe and Sharnal Street; and Beluncle, Middle Stoke, and Grain Crossing, between Sharnal Street and Port Victoria.

1910

1924

GRAVESEND (Central) and PORT VICTORIA.—Southern.

Miles.		Week Days.							Sundays.			
		mrn	mrn	mrn	aft	aft	aft	aft S	mrn	mrn	aft	aft
	Gravesend (Cen.)..dep.	6 58	7 46	1045	2 28	5 44	8 13	10 5	7 22	11 52	2 40	6 11
1	Denton Halt	7 1	7 43	1049	2 32	....	....	10 8	7 25	11 8	2 43	6 14
2¼	Milton Range Halt....	....	....	a	a	....	....	....	a	a	a	....
3¼	Uralite Halt	7 7	7 50	1057	2 41	5 52	8 20	....	7 32	1115	2 50	6 21
6	Cliffe	7 12	7 55	11 2	2 46	5 56	8 25	1018	7 37	1120	2 55	6 2[illegible]
8¼	High Halstow Halt....	7 18	8 1	11 8	2 52	6 2	8 31	1024	7 43	1126	3 1	6 33
9½	Sharnal Street ‡	7 21	8 6	1111	2 55	6 5	8 34	1027	7 46	1129	3 4	6 35
10¾	Beluncle Halt	7 25	8 11	1116	3 2	6 11	8 38	....	7 50	1133	3 8	6 39
12¼	Middle Stoke Halt	7 30	8 15	112[illegible]	3 6	6 16	8 42	....	7 54	1137	3 12	6 43
14¼	Grain Crossing Halt...	7 34	8 20	1124	3 10	6 20	8 46	....	7 58	1141	3 16	6 47
16	Port Victoria ....arr.	7 38	8 25	1128	3 14	6 24	8 51	....	8 2	1145	3 20	6 51

Miles.		Week Days.									Sundays.			
		mrn	mrn	aft S	aft E	aft	aft E	aft S	aft	aft S	mrn	aft	aft	aft
	Port Victoria ....dep.	7 48	8 55	1 5	1 10	3 34	5 10	6 45	9 6	....	8 18	1215	5 0	7 10
1¾	Grain Crossing Halt	7 52	8 59	1 11	1 14	3 38	5 14	6 49	9 10	....	8 21	1218	5 3	7 13
3¼	Middle Stoke Halt	7 58	9 3	1 16	1 18	3 42	5 18	6 53	9 14	....	8 27	1222	5 7	7 17
5¼	Beluncle Halt	8 2	9 7	1 20	1 22	3 46	5 22	6 57	9 18	....	8 31	1227	5 12	7 22
6¼	Sharnal Street ‡	8 5	9 10	1 23	1 25	3 50	5 26	7 5	9 23	1040	8 34	1234	5 16	7 26
7¾	High Halstow Halt	8 9	9 15	1 28	1 30	3 55	5 32	7 9	9 27	1043	8 38	1238	5 21	7 31
10	Cliffe	8 16	9 22	1 35	1 37	4 2	5 38	7 16	9 34	1050	8 45	1245	5 28	7 38
12¼	Uralite Halt	8 21	9 27	1 40	1 42	4 7	5 43	7 21	....	....	8 50	1250	5 33	7 43
13¼	Milton Range Halt....	....	a	a	a	....	....	....	....	....	a	a	....	....
15	Denton Halt ...[231,	....	9 35	1 48	1 50	4 16	5 48	7 27	....	....	8 57	1257	5 40	7 50
16	Gravesend (Cen.)..278, arr.	8 29	9 39	1 51	1 53	4 20	5 51	7 30	9 43	11 1	9 0	1 0	5 43	7 53

a Stop at Milton Range Halt on informing the Guard. **E** Except Saturdays. **S** Saturdays only.

‡ Station for Hoo and St. Mary's Hoo (2 miles).

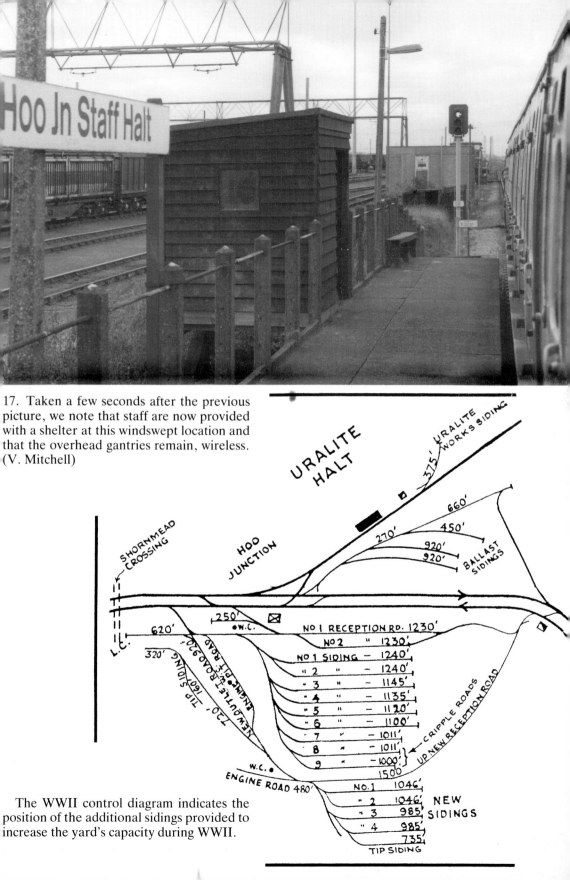

17. Taken a few seconds after the previous picture, we note that staff are now provided with a shelter at this windswept location and that the overhead gantries remain, wireless. (V. Mitchell)

The WWII control diagram indicates the position of the additional sidings provided to increase the yard's capacity during WWII.

URALITE HALT

URALITE WORKS SIDING 375'

SHORNMEAD CROSSING

HOO JUNCTION

270'
660'
450'
920'
920'
BALLAST SIDINGS

250'
• W.C.
620'
320'
L.C.
NEW OUTLET ROAD 920'
720' — TIP SIDING — 160'
NEW PIT ROAD

NO 1 RECEPTION RD. 1230'
NO 2   "   1230'
NO 1 SIDING — 1240'
" 2   "   — 1240'
" 3   "   — 1145'
" 4   "   — 1135'
" 5   "   — 1120'
" 6   "   — 1100'
" 7   "   — 1011'
8   "   — 1011'
9   "   — 1000'
1500'

CRIPPLE ROADS
UP NEW RECEPTION ROAD

W.C. •
ENGINE ROAD 480'

NO.1   1046'
" 2   1046'   NEW
" 3   985'   SIDINGS
" 4   985'
735'
TIP SIDING

URALITE HALT

18. Opened on 1st July 1906, the halt was used almost exclusively by the workers at the adjacent factory. Hoo Junction water tower is visible between the second and third railing post and the signal box is between the fourth and fifth. The factory opened in 1900 and is still in use. (Lens of Sutton)

19. The SR replaced the timber components with concrete ones and provided a shelter. H class no. 31308 was working the 3.38pm from Allhallows on 2nd September 1961 when photographed in front of the Uralite Works, which produces a corrugated roofing substitute for galvanised iron sheeting. The raw materials include asbestos fibre, from Africa and Russia, and bitumen. (J.H. Aston)

20. Apart from a short climb over the canal bridge, the branch takes a level course for one mile before a half-mile long line diverges north to the Brett gravel terminal. Four loading sidings, a cripple road and a run-round loop are provided. Marine dredged aggregates are conveyed to a number of locations, including Purley and Salfords. Between 1961 and 1969, the line was used for conveyance of cement from the APCM Cliffe Works, mainly to Glasgow. (V. Mitchell)

Summer 1958

CLIFFE

21. The station opened with the line and was provided with this typical SER timber building. A similar one has recently been restored at Ore, near Hastings. When the station closed the village had about 2250 inhabitants and was one mile to the north. (Lens of Sutton)

22. A substantial staff was required to deal with passengers, goods inward (which included coal and fertiliser), goods outward (such as milk, horticultural produce and brewers grain) and to tend to the station gardens. (Lens of Sutton)

23. Reference to the map shows that the siding in the foreground had no road access and could therefore only be used for the storage of wagons or by a goods train passing a passenger train. (Lens of Sutton)

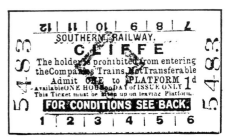

The 1908 survey shows a goods shed and crane that did not appear on the 1897 edition.

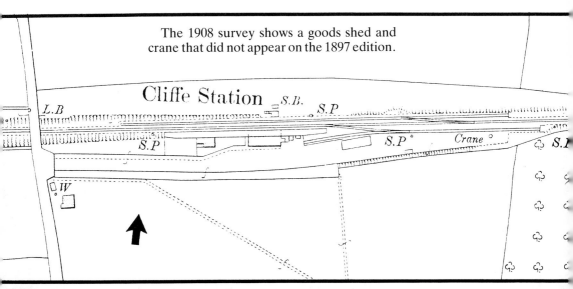

24. The signals seen in the previous picture ceased to be used on 5th December 1926 and the signal box was closed. The rods in the foreground were associated with the goods yard points. The white buffer stop of the long siding can be seen in the distance. (Lens of Sutton)

25. Class C 0–6–0 no. 31221 passes the goods yard, with its 3-ton capacity crane, on 25th August 1951. By then, the yard had an additional siding, near its southern boundary. Goods services were withdrawn on 20th August 1962, nine months after those for passengers. (D. Cullum)

26. In 1934, a passing loop was installed to increase the line's capacity in connection with the expected increase in holiday traffic. The signal box was reopened on 13th May 1934; a down platform was built and the up one refaced. (A.E. Bennett)

27. Class C no. 31223 waits in the up platform on 24th October 1953 while the ACV set appears to approach the down platform. In fact, it had reversed back from it to allow a fitter to gain access to its hidden works. These included 125 bhp AEC diesel engines, as used in Green Line coaches at that time. (R.C. Riley)

28. As the shadows lengthen on 11th September 1959, class Q1 no. 33001 blows off at the head of a train of loaded tank wagons from the refinery at Grain. Originally numbered C1, this locomotive is now to be found on the Bluebell Railway. (T. Wright)

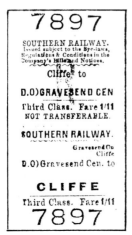

7897

SOUTHERN RAILWAY.
Issued subject to the Bye-laws,
Regulations & Conditions in the
Company's Bills and Notices.
Cliffe to
D.O)GRAVESEND CEN
Third Class. Fare 1/11
NOT TRANSFERABLE.

SOUTHERN RAILWAY.
Gravesend Cn
Cliffe
D.O)Gravesend Cen. to

CLIFFE
Third Class. Fare 1/11
7897

3rd · SINGLE   SINGLE · 3rd
0558   High Halstow Halt to   0558
HighHalstow Halt   HighHalstow Halt
Cliffe   Cliffe
CLIFFE
(S) 6d. H   FARE   6d. H (S)
For conditions see over For condition see over

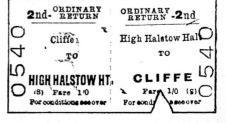

2nd- ORDINARY   ORDINARY -2nd
RETURN   RETURN
0540   Cliffe   High Halstow Halt   0540
TO   TO
HIGH HALSTOW HT.   CLIFFE
(S) Fare 1/0   Fare 1/0 (S)
For conditions see over For cond see over

29. Push-pull unit no. 616 leaves the up platform while class C no. 31592 stands with the 1.44 pm from Gravesend on 2nd September 1961. This engine is also now resident on the Bluebell Railway. The guard had to travel in the van as the solitary corridor coach (2nd class only) had no brake. (J.H. Aston)

30. No. 31592 returns from Allhallows on the same day, the photograph giving us the opportunity to see how the down platform shelter was arranged to avoid impairing the signalman's view west. The station house, on the right, was the only structure still standing in 1988. (J.H. Aston)

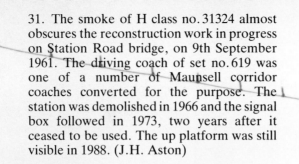

31. The smoke of H class no. 31324 almost obscures the reconstruction work in progress on Station Road bridge, on 9th September 1961. The driving coach of set no. 619 was one of a number of Maunsell corridor coaches converted for the purpose. The station was demolished in 1966 and the signal box followed in 1973, two years after it ceased to be used. The up platform was still visible in 1988. (J.H. Aston)

32. Weekend excursions to the seaside sands of Allhallows were quite popular with the residents of South London in the years before and after WWII. C class no. 31694 storms up the ¾-mile long climb at 1 in 66 to cross the "Spine of Hoo" on 10th August 1952, with one such excursion. (S.C. Nash)

34. The halt was east of the summit level and so C class no. 31495 was still climbing at 1 in 160 as she passed by on 9th July 1955, with the 3.50pm freight from Allhallows. Hot bright sun made the exhaust almost invisible. (J.H. Aston)

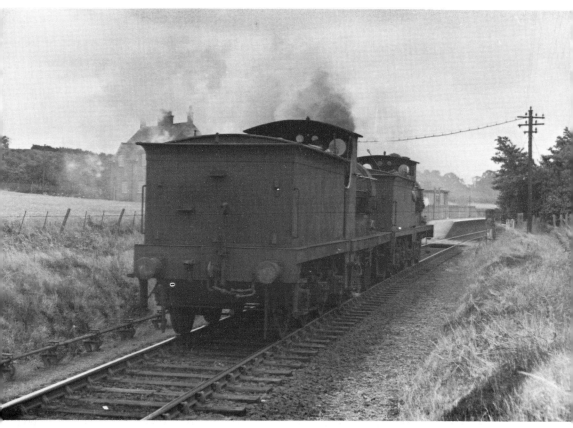

33. The village of around 400 people is about 150 ft above sea level, the halt being about ¼ mile west of the church. Excursionists know not what happened to their engines during their stay on the sands. Nos. 31086 and 31294 were coupled together to run to Gillingham Shed on 2nd August 1954. (S.C. Nash)

35. The signal box was photographed in September 1958 and remained in use until 28th September 1972, when the gates were removed and flashing lights installed. (P. Hay)

The 1897 edition does not include the halt as this did not open until 1st July 1906. It was built where the signal post (S.P.) is marked.

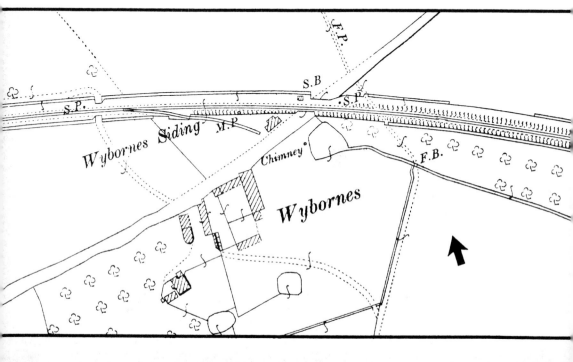

36. The third Bluebell engine to appear in this album is H class 0–4–4T no. 31263. It is seen propelling the 2.47pm from Gravesend on 9th September 1961, with its smokebox saddle endorsed "Trans Hoosey". Who cared what happened to the filthy engines, three months before closure? (J.H. Aston)

37. On the same day, the photographer waited for an hour to record the 3.50pm freight from Allhallows, which was hauled by no. D6535. Concrete cable ducts were ready to be laid so that the telegraph poles could be eliminated and modern signalling installed. (J.H. Aston)

38. To the left, the lane served a few dwellings and, to the right, it climbed to the village, from the centre of which a good bus service was available. The land rises behind the signal box and reaches a summit of 208 ft, north of the village. (A.E. Bennett)

2nd · SINGLE   SINGLE · 2nd

(D.O.) Gravesend Ctl. to (D.O.)
GravesendCentral   GravesendCentral

High Halstow Halt   High Halstow Halt

HIGH HALSTOW HALT

(S) 1/6   FARE   1/6 (S)

Vor condit'ns see over For condit'ns see over

6494   6494

39. The 2.24 pm from Allhallows passes under the bridge between Solomons Farm and its fields on 9th September 1961. Class H 0–4–4T no. 31324 is approaching milepost 32¾, while the diamond sign proclaims warnings to road engine drivers. (J.H. Aston)

40. Twenty seven years later, at almost the same location, Railfreight Sector liveried no. 33051 *Shakespeare Cliff* and no. 33050 *Isle of Grain* haul aggregates, appropriately, from the latter to the former on 29th June 1988. (B. Morrison)

SHARNAL STREET

41. Inconveniently situated nearly two miles from the village of Hoo, the station was well positioned to serve the agricultural community. Seen here on 5th June 1928, it was surrounded by fields and devoid of a down platform initially. Generous provision was made for railway staff vegetable production. (Lens of Sutton)

The 1909 edition shows the Lodge Hill line, lower left, and the earthworks ready for the Kingsnorth line, lower right.

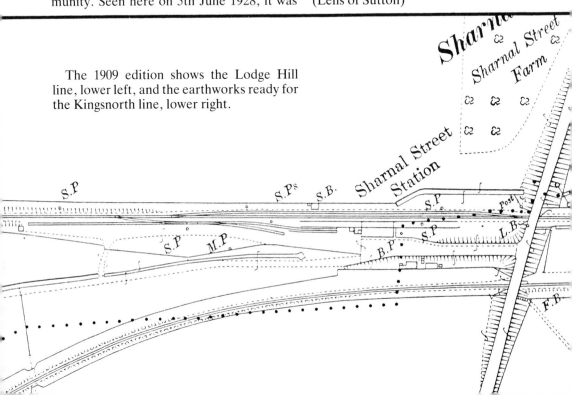

42. Another of the ubiquitous H class tanks
is seen, standing at the down platform which
was opened on 9th April 1933. Note that it
has a modern style of oil lamp.
(Lens of Sutton)

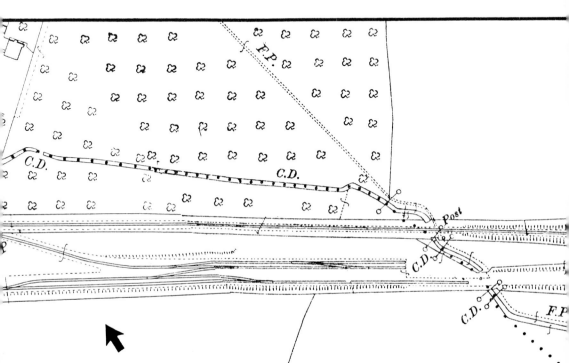

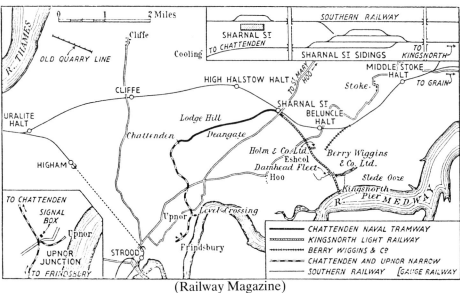

(Railway Magazine)

A standard gauge line from exchange sidings at Sharnal Street to ammunition stores at Lodge Hill was opened in 1901. It was extended to Chattenden, where it connected with the 2'6" gauge Chattenden & Upnor Railway. Royal Engineers commenced the construction of this latter line in 1899, for use by the Navy. The standard gauge line was known as the Chattenden Naval Tramway and this was extended south to Kingsnorth Pier in the early part of WWI. At the same time, the exchange sidings at Sharnal Street were extended. After the war,

Holm & Co. Ltd. established a chemical works near the line and made a connection to it in 1924. In 1929, a Light Railway Order was finalised for the Kingsnorth Light Railway and a branch laid into the works of Berry, Wiggins & Co. Ltd., who produced bitumen and oil compounds. Following a dispute, they established a direct connection to the SR in 1932. One of their locomotives is to be seen in picture 22 in our *Branch Line to Fairford*. The KLR closed during WWII and the C&UR, together with the CNT, ceased operations at the end of 1961.

←

43. A third view from the road bridge includes both foot crossings and the lamp room, or oil store, in the foreground. Class H no. 31322 propels the 2.47 pm from Graves-end on 9th July 1955. (J.H. Aston)

44. Later that afternoon, the westbound freight was recorded, along with a signalman keen to be included. No. 31495 is one of C class 0–6–0s, built between 1900 and 1908. (J.H. Aston)

45. A local train departs for Gravesend on Easter Monday 1960, as trees blossom behind the station master's house. To the left of it, the Chattenden Naval Tramway curves away to Lodge Hill. (J.J. Smith)

46. Another picture from April 1960 shows
an excursion returning to London and the
short dock siding which had been relaid with
flat-bottom rail. The chimney above the
leading coach belongs to the signal box.
(Late Derek Cross)

47. The Railway Enthusiasts Club railtour on 24th September 1960 originated at Gravesend and included Allhallows, Grain, Maidstone Goods, Chatham Dockyard, Queenborough Pier and Sheerness Dockyard. Note the station name panel in the front glass of the oil lamp. (E. Wilmshurst)

48. On 2nd September 1961, H class no. 31308 was propelling the 2.47 pm from Gravesend while no. D6516 was working the up freight service. The SER standardised on sash windows while most other companies preferred their signal box windows to slide horizontally. One window sill was severely rotted by then. (J.H. Aston)

49. Type 3 diesels were commonly used on passenger services during the last year of operation. This view of no. D6535 with the 1.06pm from Gravesend on 9th September 1961 includes the ringed shunt signal in the goods yard. (J.H. Aston)

50. Three views east from the A228 road bridge show the connection to the Chatten-den Naval Tramway. Some views of the naval lines can be seen in picture nos. 77 to 82 in *Industrial Railways of the South-East* (Middleton Press). H class no. 31308 passes over the connection on 20th October 1951 with the 2.22pm from Allhallows. Shining rails show that the sidings were then still well used. (D. Cullum)

51. C class no. 31593 hauls two empty push-pull sets past the gate to the exchange sidings on 3rd August 1953. The loop had been extended in 1933 and the down starting signal repositioned, as shown. As it was then obscured by the bridge, a banner repeater was provided on the down platform. (J.J. Smith)

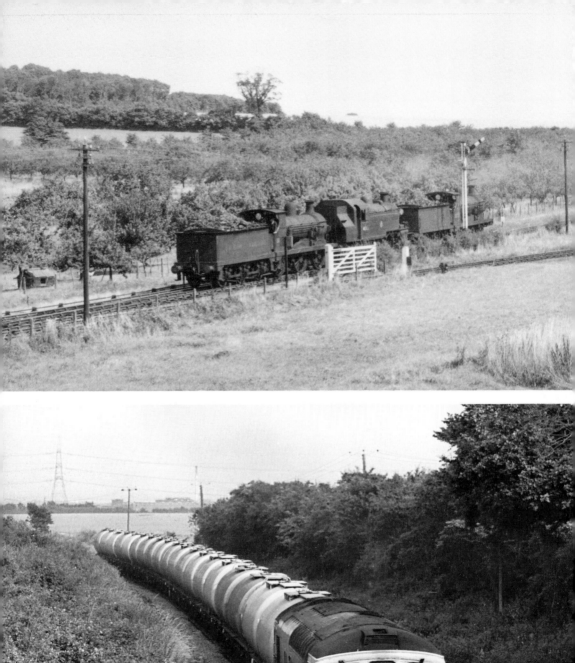

52. The Chattenden line is lower right in this photograph taken on the same day as the previous one. Excursion engines return light to Hoo Junction – C class no. 31722, having worked from Deptford, BR class 2 no. 41302 from New Cross and C class no. 31725 from Erith. (J.J. Smith)

←

53. Looking east from the bridge seen in the background of pictures 50 and 51, we witness push-pull fitted no. 33113 heading a train of loaded tankers on 29th June 1988. The pylon supports lines from Kingsnorth Power Station, which receives its coal by sea. (B. Morrison)

3r	RDINARY RETURN		ORDINARY RETURN -3rd
Allhallows on Sea			Sharnal Street
	TO		TO
SHARNAL ST.			ALLHALLOWS on SEA
(S) Fare 1/10			Fare 1/10 (S)
For conditions see over			For conditions see over

BELUNCLE HALT

54. Like the other 1906 halts, this was of timber construction and was rebuilt by the SR in concrete. The siding pre-dated the halt and was known as Miskins, after a local person involved with the line in its early days. (Lens of Sutton)

The 1909 map does not show the small building provided later, which included booking office and waiting room. A second siding was also added.

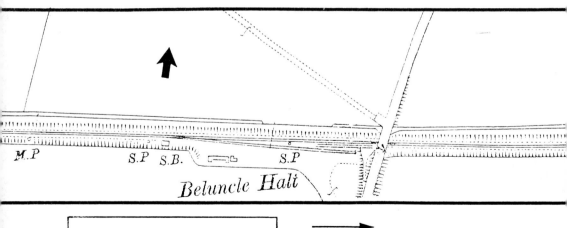

56. Class Q1 no. 33032 passes the staff cottage on 18th April 1960, hauling push-pull set no. 716 from Gravesend. It was not equipped to push the coaches back, this class having been built for freight work. (J.J. Smith)

55. The halt was named after Beluncle Farm, which was almost the nearest building, ¼ mile south of the line. The numerous pipes and most of the five hoses were provided in association with the pneumatically operated push-pull equipment, as were the pipe descriptions painted on the buffer beam. (P. Hay)

MIDDLE STOKE HALT

57. Of the 1906 halts, this was one of the most useful being fairly close to habitation, as can be seen in this northward view. Behind the camera is marshland leading to Stoke Ooze. (Lens of Sutton)

58. Type 3 diesel no. D6516 throbs along the deserted concrete platform on 2nd September 1961, with the 1.06pm from Gravesend. Stoke is ½ mile east of Middle Stoke and the larger Lower Stoke, ½ mile to the north. Residents had petitioned unsuccessfully for a station soon after the line opened. (J.H. Aston)

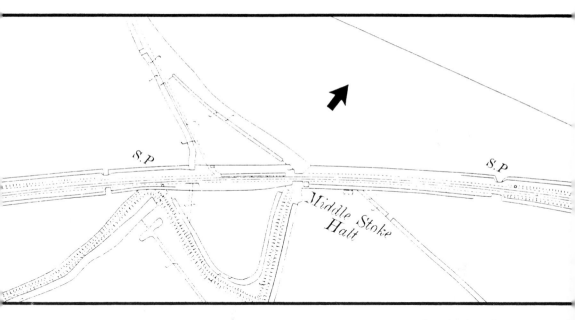

The 1908 survey reveals that the lane from the village terminated at the line and that a footpath led to the platform.

59. The photographer's sons give the impression of passengers on 9th September 1961, as H class no. 31324 runs in with the 12.20 pm from Allhallows. The platform lamps were removed from the board when not in use. (J.H. Aston)

STOKE JUNCTION HALT

60. The halt opened two months after the Allhallows branch on 17th July 1932 and was close to Stoke crossing on the main road to Grain. A photograph from 30th March 1959 shows the 4.53pm from Allhallows approaching, the BP refinery being visible in the background. (J.J. Smith)

61. The small signal box doubled up as a goods office and became a block post after the opening of the branch. The gates were opened by hand and were replaced by flashing lights on 28th September 1972. (Lens of Sutton)

62. A Maidstone & District bus is held up by the 12.20 pm from Allhallows on 2nd September 1961, the single coach of which is devoid of a brake compartment, necessitating a van at the rear. C class no. 31592 has an unwilling injector, a problem experienced by your author (VM) while firing the locomotive on the Bluebell Railway.
(J.H. Aston)

0098

SOUTHERN RAILWAY.
Issued subject to the Bye-laws,
Regulations & Conditions in the
Company's Bill's and Notices

Cheap Day as advertised

to STOKE JC HALT
Via

Third Class

NOT TRANSFERABLE

SOUTHERN RAILWAY.
CHEAP DAY
Stoke Jc. Halt to

Via

Third Class

0098

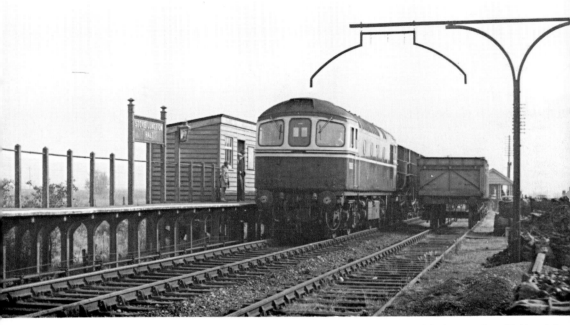

63. The siding is shown on the 1908 survey and was probably opened with the line, latterly being used mainly by a local coal merchant. No. D6535 passes through with mineral wagons on 9th September 1961, with genuine passengers waiting for the following service. (J.H. Aston)

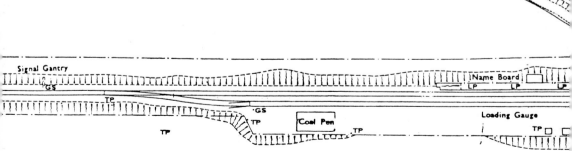

Signal Gantry

Name Board

Coal Pen

Loading Gauge

1956 plan at 1:2500 scale

64. Lower Stoke was over ½ mile from the halt and can be seen in the right background. It had a population of about 600, prior to WWII. The small building included an operational booking office in earlier days. (A.E. Bennett)

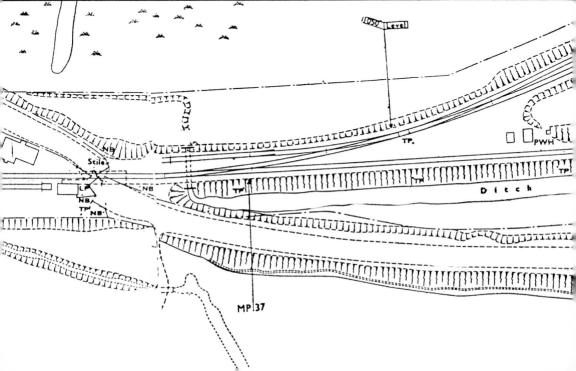

65. Class 0-6-0 no. 31223 takes the straight line towards Grain on 24th October 1953, the sharply curved line to Allhallows passing behind the permanent way hut. Lack of a turntable at Gravesend at this time necessitated tender first running. (D. Cullum)

66. The 3.20pm from Allhallows reaches the end of the double track section on 2nd August 1954, hauled by H class no. 31158. The line was single initially and a loop was provided here. The branch was doubled on 1st July 1934 and was singled again in 1957. (S.C. Nash)

67. A westward view in July 1958 shows the new sand drag to catch any over-runs from the Allhallows branch, the curve of which was subject to a 10mph speed restriction. The mile long Yantlet siding made a trailing connection to the Grain line, in the distance. This served a gun testing establishment during and after both world wars.
(A.E. Bennett)

68. Severe flooding of the East Coast in 1953 resulted in train services being suspended between 31st January and 2nd March. The refinery was subsequently protected by flood banks and this necessitated the installation of flood gates, west of Grain level crossing. This is the eastward view in March 1959.
(J.J. Smith)

GRAIN HALT

69. The halt was opened in 1906 for the benefit of the 500 or so villagers of Grain, whose dwellings were two miles to the north. Although the station at Port Victoria was just as near, it had no road access. A Q class 0–4–4T approaches with an up train in about 1915. (Lens of Sutton)

71. This is the westward view, shortly before the halt ceased to be used after 6th June 1951. It was replaced by a two platform station, 400 yards to the east, on 3rd September 1951. (J.J. Smith)

1942

GRAVESEND CENTRAL and PORT VICTORIA

Miles	Down.	Week Days. mrn	mrn	mrn	mrn	mrn		SO	SX	SO	SO		SX	SO	SX		SO	SX	SO	SX		SX	SO	SX	SO	Sundays. mrn		mrn	mrn		aft		aft	aft
	Gravesend Cen ¶ dp	5 26	6 38	..	9 4	1015	..	12[illegible]	1 0	1 10	2 16	..	2 3[illegible]	2 45	4 14	..	4 2[illegible]	5 39	6 4	6 8	..	7 45	8 2	8 52	9 33	7 0	..	9 13	1110	..	2 6	..	4 6	7 10
5¼	Cliffe ¶	5 38	6 51	..	9 17	1030	..	1244	1 11	1 21	2 27	..	2 45	2 58	4 27	..	4 45	5 52	6 1[illegible]	6 19	..	7 56	8 15	9 4	9 46	7 13	..	9 26	1123	..	2 20	..	4 20	7 24
9¼	Sharnal Street C ¶	5 45	6 59	n	9 25	1038	..	1252	1 19	1 28	2 34	..	2 53	3 6	4 35	..	4 53	6 0	6 25	6 26	..	8 4	8 23	9 13	9 54	7 21	..	9 34	1131	..	2 28	..	4 28	7 32
13	Stoke Junc. Halt ¶	5 52	7 11	7 49	9 36	1049	..	1 3	1 26	1 35	2 41	..	3 12	3 17	4 46	..	5 4	6 11	6 36	6 33	..	8 11	8 34	9 24	10 5	7 32	..	9 45	1142	..	2 39	..	4 39	7 43
14¼	Allhallows A arr.	5 56	..	7 57	9 41	1053	..	1 8	1 31	1 39	2 46	..	3 16	3 21	..	..	5 8	6 16	6 41	6 38	..	8 15	8 39	9 29	1010	7 37	..	9 50	1147	..	2 44	..	4 44	7 48
15¼	Port Victoria .. "	..	7 19	..	..	..	..	..	..	..	..	..	..	..	4 53	..	..	..	..	..	..	..	..	..	..	..	..	..	..	..	..	..	..	..

Miles	Miles	Up.	Week Days. mrn	mrn	mrn		mrn	mrn	mrn SX	mrn SO	SO		aft	aft SO	aft SX	aft SO		SX	aft SO	aft		aft	aft SX	aft SO	Sundays. mrn		mrn		non	aft		aft	aft
		Port Victoria ¶ ..dep.	..	..	7 40	..	..	..			122[illegible]	..	..				..	5 5		..	..	..			..	..	..	..	..	..	..	..	..
—		Allhallows A .. "	6 [illegible]	7 14	..	..	8 3	9 48	1120	1145	..	..	1 40	2 17	3 22	3 37	..	..	5 17	6 50	..	8 56	9 39	1015	8 2	..	10 0	..	12 0	2 51	..	4 52	8 20
2¼	1¼	Stoke Junction Halt ¶	6 6	7 18	7 49	..	8 7	9 52	1124	1149	1239	..	1 43	2 21	3 26	3 41	..	5 11	5 21	6 54	..	9 0	9 43	1019	8 6	..	10 4	..	12 4	2 55	..	4 56	8 24
6¼	5¼	Sharnal Street C ¶	6 14	7 29	h	..	8 18	10 4	1135	12 0	1250	..	1 50	2 2[illegible]	3 37	3 52	..	5 2[illegible]	5 32	7 5	..	9 10	9 54	1030	8 17	..	1015	..	1215	3 6	..	5 7	8 35
10	9	Cliffe ¶ ......[371	6 24	7 37	..	..	8 26	1013	1141	12 6	1 2	..	1 58	2 41	3 45	4 0	..	5 30	5 40	7 13	..	9 18	10 2	1038	8 25	..	1023	..	1223	3 14	..	5 15	8 43
15¼	14¼	Gravesend C. 348, arr.	6 [illegible]	7 50	..	..	8 40	10[illegible]	1154	1220	1 17	..	2 12	2 55	4 0	4 15	..	5 45	5 54	7 25	..	9 30	1014	1050	8 39	..	1037	..	1237	3 29	..	5 30	8 59

←

70. The rustic timber structure was replaced by standard pre-cast components, manufactured at the SR's works at Exmouth Junction. This view dates from around 1935. (Lens of Sutton)

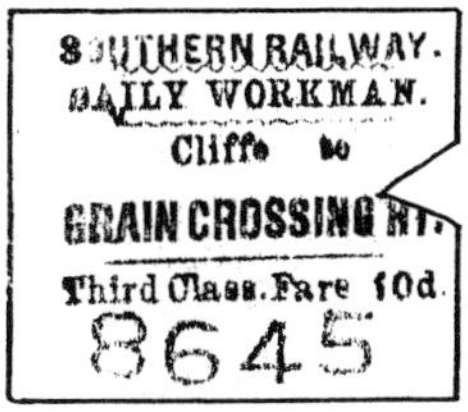
SOUTHERN RAILWAY.
DAILY WORKMAN.
Cliffe to
GRAIN CROSSING HT.
Third Class. Fare 10d.
8645

72. Electro-diesel no. 73127 returns with Chipman's weed killing train on 17th May 1986, passing the site of the halt which was on the left. The gates were opened by hand and a green flag used in place of the inoperable signal. (B. Morrison)

GRAIN

74. Although the new platforms came into use on 3rd September 1951, the signal box was still incomplete when photographed on 24th October 1953. A temporary hut had been provided for the key token instrument which was transferred from Port Victoria. (D. Cullum)

73. Looking west from the BR boundary in August 1988, it is difficult to see the trailing connection to the bitumen sidings, which is in front of the gas holder and on the route of the former Yantlet siding. Earlier, a triangular junction had connected this part of the BP railway network to BR. (V. Mitchell)

In 1923, the Medway Oil and Storage Company established a depot for the distribution of oil products, imported mainly from the USA. The siding to it was simply known as *MOSCO*. The firm became part of the Power Petroleum Co. which was absorbed by British Petroleum (BP). In 1948, work started on a massive refinery for BP and eventually 6½ miles of railway siding was laid within its boundaries. The Royal Train came to Grain on 5th April 1955, carrying HM Queen Elizabeth II, who performed the official opening. This diagram shows the track layout in 1978.

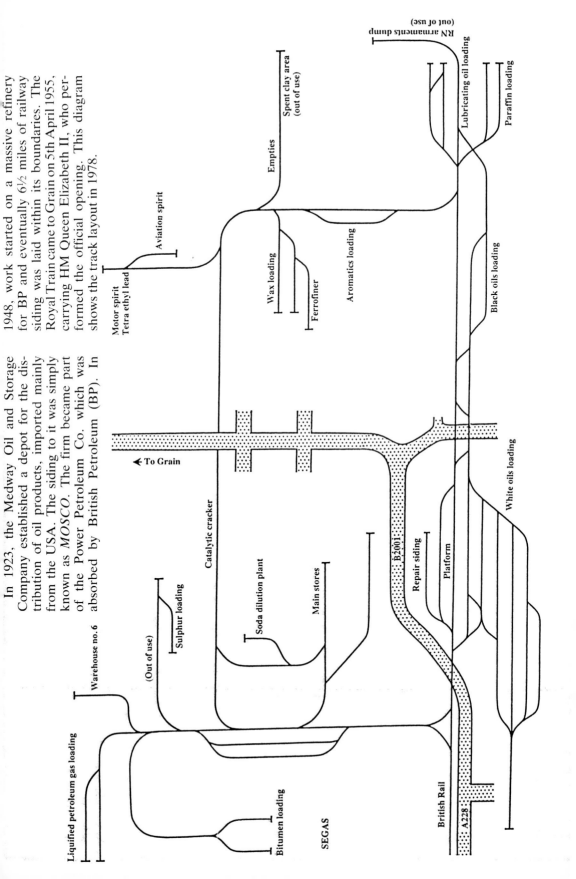

Private and not for Circulation.   (No. 25 S.T.)

South Eastern and Chatham Railway.

To the Officers and Servants of this and other Companies concerned.

INSTRUCTIONS TO

STATION MASTERS, INSPECTORS, ENGINEMEN, GUARDS, SIGNALMEN, PLATE-LAYERS, GATEMEN, AND ALL OTHERS CONCERNED

AS TO

A SPECIAL TRAIN

CONVEYING

Their Majesties

King George V. and Queen Mary

AND SUITES.

VICTORIA TO PORT VICTORIA.

On Monday, May 19th, 1913.

TIME TABLE—DOWN JOURNEY.

Distance from Victoria.		STATION or JUNCTION.	Royal Train.	
			P.M.	
M.	C.		arr.	dep.
—	—	**VICTORIA** (*No. 9 Departure Platform*)	—	6 0
0	70	Battersea Pier Junction	6	2½
1	66	Factory Junction..................................	6	4
3	14	Brixton	6	6½
3	59	Loughboro' Junction	6	7½
5	59	Elephant & Castle	6	11
6	42	Blackfriars Junction (No. 1 Road)	6 13½	—
6	42	Blackfriars Junction (No. 1 Road)	—	6 16½
6	67	Metropolitan Junction	6	18
7	30	London Bridge....................................	6	19½
8	25	Spa Road	6	21½
9	6	Southwark Park	6	23
10	34	New Cross	6	25
11	7	St. John's	6	26
11	51	Park's Bridge Junction	6	27
12	52	Hither Green Junction	6	28½
22	48	Dartford (20 miles an hour)	6	42
29	33	Gravesend Central (Through Road)............	6	51
32	55	Hoo Junction	6	56
35	38	Cliffe	7	0
38	64	Sharnal Street	7	5
45	27	**PORT VICTORIA**	7 15	—

Train to run upon the Metropolitan Line, Loughboro' Junction to Blackfriars Junction, and on No. 3 Down Line, London Bridge to Southwark Park Junction, thence via the Spur Line, crossing from Down Main to Down Local at Park's Bridge Junction Cabin.

Speed must be reduced when passing through the Facing Points at Brixton Junction, Blackfriars Junction, Metropolitan Junction, Borough Market Junction, London Bridge "A," "B" and "C" Cabins Signals and Hoo Junction.

A **Turn-over Engine will be provided and will be stationed in readiness on the Turn-Table in the Up Goods Siding at Blackfriars Junction from 5.30 p.m., and immediately the Royal Train has been brought to a stand with the rear Vehicle clear of the Turn-Table Points, this Turn-over Engine will be backed on to the Royal Train and work it away at once to Port Victoria.**

Single Line Working.—The Train Staff working on the Hundred of Hoo Branch will be in charge of Chief-Inspector GREENSTREET, at Hoo Junction.

Additional Block Signalling Section.—Stoke Siding Box (between Sharnal Street and Port Victoria) will be opened as an additional Block Signalling Section from **6.30 p.m.** and until the Return Special Train has cleared. Mr. HAYTER to arrange.

FORMATION OF TRAIN.

FORMATION OF DOWN TRAIN LEAVING VICTORIA.—Engine, 1 Bogie Brake Saloon (No. 2,301), 1 Bogie Saloon (No. 3,514), 1 Bogie Saloon (No. 3,786), **The Royal Saloon**, 1 Bogie Corridor First (No. 225), 1 Bogie Brake Saloon (No. 3,493).

The Chief Engineer, the Superintendent of the Line, and the Locomotive Running Superintendent will travel with the Train.

75. Two photographs from 9th July 1955 show the 11.50 am (Saturdays only) departure for Gravesend. On Mondays to Fridays, the only passenger train left at 5.12 pm. There was one arrival from Gravesend at 7.14 am. (J.H. Aston)

77. Access to the BP lines was through the gate beyond the PW hut, above which two of the company's 0–6–0 diesel shunters are partly visible. There were two Hunslets and a Barclay. The original *MOSCO* siding had entered the site from the opposite direction. (J.J. Smith)

76. The lengthy platforms were intended for use by refinery workers but they mainly preferred to travel by road. The crossing cottage is seen in the distance and some of the BP sidings are beyond the fence on the left. (J.H. Aston)

79. On 21st March 1970, the RCTS railtour originated at Clapham Junction and was composed of DEMUs 6L no. 1033 and 2H no. 1119. While passenger traffic to Grain had been light, oil trains increased in number and weight. (S.C. Nash)

78. The last passenger train is seen leaving at 11.37 am on Saturday 2nd December 1961. It was formed of push-pull set no. 609 and class H 0–4–4T no. 31324. The advanced starting signal had failed and so the signalman is using a flag. Note the platform indicator below the down signals. (J.J. Smith)

80. Some 1988 views of the former refinery site now follow, from west to east. The overgrown 1951 platform and PW hut are now BP property and the gateway no longer has any meaning. The entire site is bonded and public access is not possible. (V. Mitchell)

2nd · SINGLE

London Bridge **to**

ALLHALLOWS·ON·SEA

Via Gravesend Central

(S) 3/1 **FARE** 3/1 (S)

for condit... see over

0164 0164

2nd · SINGLE   SINGLE · 2nd

Charing Cross To

Charing Cross   Charing Cross
Allhallows-on-S.   Allhallows-on-S.

ALLHALLOWS·ON·SEA

Via Gravesend Cen.

(S) 6/6 **FARE** 6/6 (S)

For condit'ns see over   it'ns see over

1187 1187

81. *Kentish Maid* is one of two Rolls Royce engined diesel shunters built by Thomas Hill for BP and is seen here by her fuel tank at the west end of the site. Tankers are loaded with petrol and aviation spirit in this area. *Man of Kent* is used for shunting bitumen tankers arriving from Cardiff. (V. Mitchell)

SOUTHERN RAILWAY.
PRIVILEGE TICKET.
Available for One Week
including Day of Issue.

Slades Green
Allhallows-on-Sea

Slades Green to

ALLHALLOWS on SEA

Third Class

0642

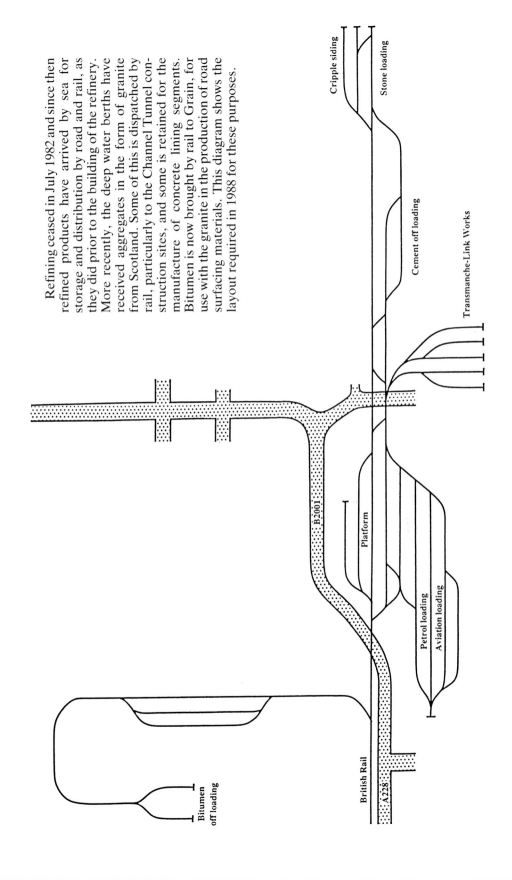

Refining ceased in July 1982 and since then refined products have arrived by sea for storage and distribution by road and rail, as they did prior to the building of the refinery. More recently, the deep water berths have received aggregates in the form of granite from Scotland. Some of this is dispatched by rail, particularly to the Channel Tunnel construction sites, and some is retained for the manufacture of concrete lining segments. Bitumen is now brought by rail to Grain, for use with the granite in the production of road surfacing materials. This diagram shows the layout required in 1988 for these purposes.

Cripple siding

Stone loading

Cement off loading

Transmanche-Link Works

B2001

Platform

Petrol loading

Aviation loading

Bitumen off loading

British Rail

A228

82. Looking west along no. 5 road, we see the petrol loading siding on the left and tunnel segments on the right. These were produced nearby in 1972 for the previous abortive attempt to create the Channel Tunnel. (V. Mitchell)

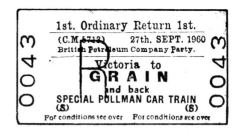

83. In 1986, Transmanche Link commenced construction of a works for the production of concrete segments for lining the Channel Tunnels. Foster Yeoman ship in the necessary aggregates from their Glensanda Quarry at Morven, near Oban, while Blue Circle provide the cement from their Northfleet Works. Two or three train loads arrive each week. The roads of the former refinery are in the foreground, while ships discharge petroleum products in the background. (TML Joint Venture)

84. Corruthers portal cranes span the yard which is used for segment storage and curing, the latter taking 10 to 14 days. Up to 21 trains per week are planned, in order to meet tunnel construction requirements. Unexpectedly difficult geological conditions can necessitate the use of cast iron segments and suddenly reduce the demand for concrete ones. (TML Joint Venture)

85. On 23rd March 1988, Mr. David Mitchell, then Minister of Transport, performed the official opening of the plant and no. 34016 *Bodmin* was brought by road from the Mid-Hants Railway for the occasion. Adjacent to the portal crane running rail in the foreground is a plastic protected electric conductor rail, with underside contact. (TML Joint Venture)

2nd SINGLE-SINGLE 2nd

High Halstow Halt to

High Halstow Halt   High Halstow Halt
Grain   Grain

GRAIN

(S) 1/2   FARE   1/2 (S)

For conditions see over   For conditions see over

2nd - SINGLE   SINGLE - 2nd

Grain to

Grain   Grain

Stoke Jc. Halt   Stoke Jc. Halt

STOKE JUNCTION HALT

(S)   4d.   FARE   4d.   (S)

For condit'ns see over   For condit'ns see over

86. A view east towards the end of the line shows the hoppers of a tarmac production plant and bogie cement tankers. Ready mixed concrete is distributed by road from the site. (V. Mitchell)

87. Looking west from a point close to the end of the line and near the site of Port Victoria station, we see the fuel storage tanks and cement silos. The wagon on the right is standing in the cripple siding. (V. Mitchell)

PORT VICTORIA

88. The SER gained royal consent for the use of the Queen's name for their new cross-channel port, it being important to equal or better the rival LCDR's Queenborough on the opposite shore. The terminus became popular with royalty, as it was remote from the public gaze. (Lens of Sutton)

89. On the left is the "temporary" wooden hotel, which lasted from 1882 until 1952 and was initially leased by Simonds, brewers of Reading, at the extreme west end of the SER system. Minimal facilities were provided on the basis that more could be provided if traffic developed. (Lens of Sutton)

90. In the early years, the mail boat to Flushing (Vlissingen) sailed twice daily and there was a regular service across the river to Sheerness, connecting with local trains. Until silting took place there was a minimum of 16 ft. of water at low tide by the pier. (Lens of Sutton)

The 1908 survey confirms that there was no road access to the terminus. The centre of the three tracks was the running line, the one on the left being a siding and the other leading to the turntable.

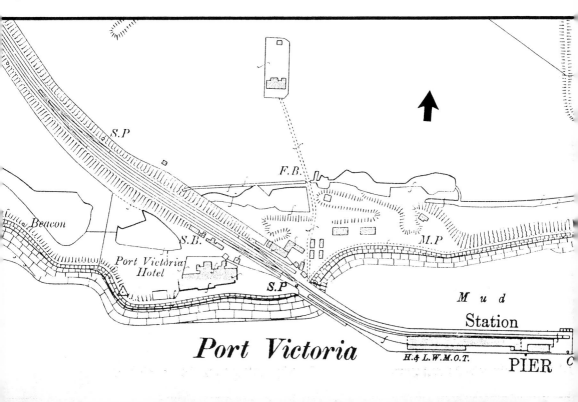

91. Heavy repairs to the timber pier were carried out in 1897–98 and it was declared unsafe again in 1916. Thereafter, trains terminated at the shore end of the platform, but the buildings remained in use as offices. This is the scene in 1928. (Lens of Sutton)

92. With the hotel in the background, class H no. A311 stands on the pier on 26th April 1930. The following year, trains were banned from the structure entirely, although the timber supports had been earlier cased with concrete. (H.C. Casserley)

93. The buffer stops were moved progressively inland, the next move from this being onto firm land. Lighting of the platform presented problems due to the strength of the wind and so Duplex paraffin lamps were provided. (Lens of Sutton)

0030

SOUTHERN RAILWAY.

This ticket is issued subject to the Company's Bye-laws, Regulations & Conditions in their Time Tables, Notices and Book of Regulations. Available on Day of issue only.

THIRD CLASS SINGLE
Fare 2/-
BETWEEN

PORT VICTORIA (G.C.
AND
GRAVESEND CENTRAL

Passenger requested to see ticket punched when issued

Port Victoria
TO
DARTFORD
First Class.
002

94. In 1931, this timber platform was built but it was devoid of the obligatory ramp at the shore end. The generous triple track arrangement was retained. (Lens of Sutton)

96. The remains of the pier were photographed on the same day, with Sheerness and
Queenborough visible on the far shore of the
Medway Estuary, which is slightly over one
mile wide at this point. (J.H. Aston)

95. The 5.05 pm departure
is viewed from the signal
box on 11th September
1947, with 3rd class clearly
emphasised on every
door. There was one pas-
senger, in addition to the
photographer.
(J.H. Aston)

97. The 45 ft. turntable was ⅓ mile from the shore and by 1947 the remains of the lamp looked of more use to announce the arrival of the Armada. The opening of the line had been delayed by two months owing to the Board of Trade insisting on the provision of a turntable here. (J.H. Aston)

98. Passenger services ceased on 11th June 1951 and three photographs taken shortly afterwards show the state of neglect. On the left is the weed covered line from the turntable and beyond the crossover a siding curves to the left to a naval arms dump. The adjacent marshes were reclaimed for extension of the refinery. (J.J. Smith)

TRAIN SERVICE TO AND FROM PORT VICTORIA.
TUESDAY, APRIL 17th, and until further notice.

DOWN TRAINS—WEEK DAYS.

STATIONS.	a m	a m	S p m	NS p m	S p m	S p m	NS p m	S p m	NS p m	p m	S p m		
Charing Cross ....dep.	6 0	9 40	1 25	1 30	2 27	4 35	..	5 25	..	7 7	*8 30	..	..
Waterloo .... „	6 2	9 42	1 27	1 32	2 29	..	..	..	..	7 9	*8 32	..	..
Cannon Street .... „	6 0	*9 34	*1 24	*1 12	2 36	4 43	4 43	5 34	5 37	7 16	8 55	..	..
London Bridge .... „	6 16	9 48	1 32	1 37	2 39	..	..	5 37	5 40	7 19	8 58	..	..
Gravesend Central .... arr.	7 24	10 50	2 16	2 17	3 24	5 20	5 24	6 17	6 25	8 3	9 44	..	..
Gravesend Central ....dep.	8 26	11 12	2 25	2 25	3 35	5 27	5 30	6 38	6 38	8 12	9 55	..	..
Cliffe .... „	8 37	11 23	2 36	2 36	3 46	5 37	5 40	6 49	6 49	8 22	10 6	..	..
Sharnal Street .... arr.	8 44	11 30	2 43	2 43	3 52	5 43	5 45	6 56	6 56	8 23	10 12	..	..
Port Victoria .... „	8 56	11 42	2 56	2 56	4 4	5 55	5 58	7 8	7 8	8 40	..	..	

UP TRAINS—WEEK DAYS.

STATIONS.	a m	a m	NS p m	S p m	S p m	NS p m	S p m	p m	S p m (May and June only)	p m (May and June only)	S p m
Port Victoria ....dep.	8 4	9 12	1 4	1 14	3 1	3 3	4 46	6 14	7 54	9 0	..
Sharnal Street............. arr.	8 16	9 23	1 15	1 26	3 13	3 16	4 57	6 25	8 4	9 12	10 20
Cliffe .... dep.	8 25	9 29	1 24	1 33	3 19	3 22	5 4	6 32	8 10	9 20	10 26
Gravesend Central .... arr.	8 37	9 40	1 35	1 46	3 30	3 32	5 15	6 43	8 22	9 31	10 37
Gravesend Central ....dep.	8 48	9 51	1 49	1 56	3 59	3 59	6 3	7 16	8 36	9 50	10 37
London Bridge .... arr.	9 23	10 26	2 51	2 53	4 44	4 44	6 41	8 15	9 24	10 43	12 15
Cannon Street .... „	9 27	10 30	2 57	3 0	4 48	4 48	..	8 21	9 30	10 54	12 21
Waterloo .... „	..	..	..	..	..	..	6 45	8 25	...	..	12 25
Charing Cross............. „	..	..	..	..	..	..	6 50	8 29	...	..	12 29

S Saturdays only.   **NS** Not on Saturdays.   * Change at London Bridge.

99. A view from the top of the up starting signal includes the signal box, locomotive water tank and the Station Hotel. The line subsequently became a long siding from Grain and eventually part of the BP system. (J.J. Smith)

100. The concrete platform carried few passengers, having been erected less than two years before closure. The line climbed at 1 in 800 for ¼ mile before entering the station area. A pipe valve is in the foreground while the refinery rises in the background. (J.J. Smith)

ALLHALLOWS-ON-SEA

101. Work commenced on the 1¾ mile long branch in August 1929 and the first excursions arrived on Saturday 14th May 1932, scheduled services commencing the following week. The contractor's Manning Wardle 0–6–0ST and tipper wagons are seen on the right. (Lens of Sutton)

The 1938 map at 6″ to 1 mile emphasises the extreme isolation of the terminus on Allhallows Marshes, "Mud" representing the position of the beach, just downstream from the sewer outfall.

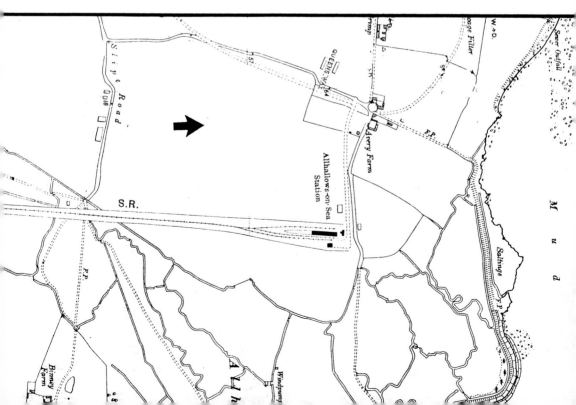

102. Initially only one platform, with a short awning, was provided. There were two sidings, one of which was connected to the platform line for running round purposes. (Lens of Sutton)

103. A third photograph from 1932 was taken before the completion of the wiring of the short-lived fence and the erection of platform lights. The headcode indicated North Kent line via Blackheath.
(Lens of Sutton)

104. The milk churns give a rural flavour to this SR outpost, which was under 39 miles from Charing Cross. The suffix *ON SEA* was open to question, as the village is on the Thames Estuary, one mile within the boundary of the Port of London Authority. (D. Cullum collection)

105. Prior to WWII, visitors had the benefit of a miniature railway to reduce the length of the long walk to the beach. In the background is the roof of the large goods shed. (Lens of Sutton)

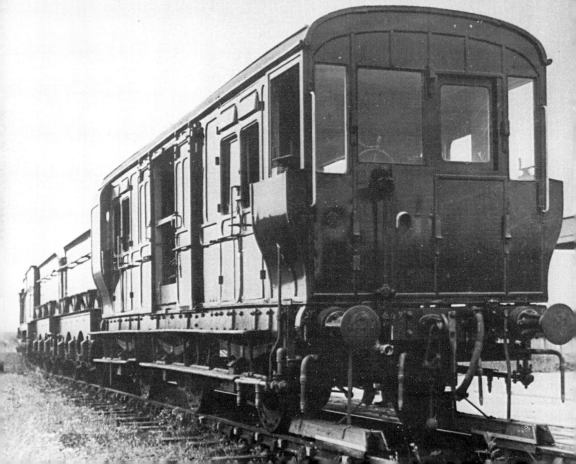

106. A second platform was brought into use on 10th April 1933 and a longer, full width, steel canopy erected. White bands were painted on the nameboard posts during the blackout of WWII. (Lens of Sutton)

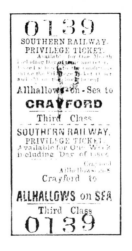

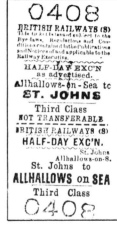

SOUTHERN RAILWAY.
PRIVILEGE TICKET.
Available for One Month
including Day of Issue and not
transferable to the conditions
under the Privilege Ticket Order
and Notices in respect thereof
Allhallows-on-Sea to
CRAYFORD
Third Class
SOUTHERN RAILWAY.
PRIVILEGE TICKET
Available for One Week
including Day of Issue
Crayford and
Allhallows-on-S
Crayford to
ALLHALLOWS on SEA
Third Class
0139

BRITISH RAILWAYS (S)
This ticket is issued subject to the
Bye-laws, Regulations and Con-
ditions contained in the Publications
and Notices of and applicable to the
Railway Executive.
HALF-DAY EXC'N
as advertised.
Allhallows-on-Sea to
ST. JOHNS
Third Class
NOT TRANSFERABLE
BRITISH RAILWAYS (S)
HALF-DAY EXC'N.
St. Johns
Allhallows-on-S.
St. Johns to
ALLHALLOWS on SEA
Third Class

107. The 1937 weed killing train is seen in no. 2 siding. The old locomotive tenders supplied water to mix with the chemicals in the ex-SECR PBV van. Note the shields to protect the running rails from the spray nozzles. (British Rail)

108. R class 0–4–4T no. 1659 waits to leave at 1.40 pm on 11th September 1947. In the background is the asbestos roofed and clad goods shed, which was dismantled in about 1950. (J. H. Aston)

109. Nine coach set no. 897 was hopefully packed with contented day-trippers, returning at 5.47pm on 3rd August 1953. R class no. 31660 blows off as it approaches the outer home, ready to start its straight level run to Stoke Junction following a slight descent from the terminus. (J.J. Smith)

110. The flats in the background (Albany Court) stand as a monument to the hopes of the property developers and the SR who expected big profits from the area. Class D no. 31488 waits to depart at 11.18am, with two push-pull sets, on 6th August 1951. (J.J. Smith)

111. The ACV set had bodywork by Park Royal and is seen on 31st October 1953. Previous trials that year had been between Marylebone and High Wycombe; on the Amlwch branch; in the Ayr district; in the Midlands and on the Southminster branch. BR purchased the cars in November and put them to work between Watford and St. Albans. (S.C. Nash)

112. The 4.45 pm departure on 5th August 1957 was formed of 6-set no. 900, complete with "Birdcages", while other stock stands in the sidings. Class C no. 31293 passes milepost 38½, where a ¼ mile descent at 1 in 220 commenced. (J.J. Smith)

113. While a conventional push-pull set stood behind class H no. 31308 on 31st August 1958, two former steam railmotor coaches were stabled in the siding in the background. The glazed area of the canopy is evident in this view. (P. Hay)

114. The SR poster board was still standing in 1959, partly obscured by the timetable of Maidstone & District Motor Services. From 1930 to 1960, the population increased from 330 to 580, a nightmare for those who dreamed of another Westcliff or Southend arising on the marshes. (J.J. Smith)

115. The full extent of the railway yard and the main buildings of the pre-war development are revealed in this photograph from August 1959. Beyond the station is *The Pilot*, a public house now largely surrounded by caravan parks. On the right is the line to the 50 ft. turntable. (Pamlin Prints)

116. Another 1959 view shows the paint peeling and mouldings rotting. It also shows the boundary between the original and later canopies. Class H no. 31519 is coupled to former railmotor cars forming set no. 481. The station came under the jurisdiction of Cliffe station master. (T. Wright)

117. A month from closure, the guard was again obliged to travel in a four-wheeled parcel van, as only a SK and a BY were available. The driver oils up his C class, unaware that it would be the only member of its class to be preserved. (J.H. Aston)

1:1250

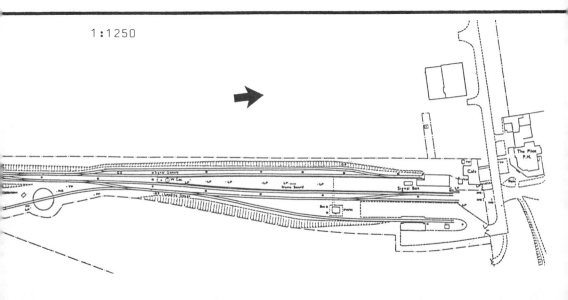

118. No. D6553 leaves with the final goods train on 2nd December 1961, the turntable being evident on the right. Freight traffic had been minimal, shingle being the main commodity to leave. The locomotive is crossing to the down line, as the up one had been taken out of use in 1957. (J.J. Smith)

119. With *The Pilot* on the skyline, a small crowd gathers to watch H class no. 31324 take water on the penultimate working day. Official closure was Monday 4th December 1961. The entire site is now occupied by caravans. (A.E. Bennett)

120. Photographers line up to record the last passenger train departure at 8.38 pm on 3rd December 1961. The grimy locomotive was C class no. 31689. After a life of less than 30 years, the station had only seen crowds for a few summer weekends in the pre and post-war years and is now but a memory recorded only in photographs. (R. Joanes)

Other photographs of the area are to be found in Peter Hay's *Steaming through Kent.* (Middleton Press)

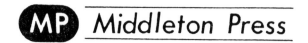

MP Middleton Press

Easebourne Lane, Midhurst, West Sussex, GU29 9AZ
☎ Midhurst (073 081) 3169

BRANCH LINES
BRANCH LINES TO MIDHURST
BRANCH LINES TO HORSHAM
BRANCH LINES TO EAST GRINSTEAD
BRANCH LINES TO ALTON
BRANCH LINE TO HAYLING
BRANCH LINE TO SOUTHWOLD
BRANCH LINE TO TENTERDEN
BRANCH LINES TO NEWPORT
BRANCH LINES TO TUNBRIDGE WELLS
BRANCH LINE TO SWANAGE
BRANCH LINES TO LONGMOOR
BRANCH LINES TO LYME REGIS
BRANCH LINES **AROUND** MIDHURST
BRANCH LINE TO FAIRFORD
BRANCH LINE TO ALLHALLOWS

SOUTH COAST RAILWAYS
BRIGHTON TO WORTHING
CHICHESTER TO PORTSMOUTH
BRIGHTON TO EASTBOURNE
RYDE TO VENTNOR
EASTBOURNE TO HASTINGS
PORTSMOUTH TO SOUTHAMPTON
HASTINGS TO ASHFORD*
SOUTHAMPTON TO BOURNEMOUTH
ASHFORD TO DOVER
BOURNEMOUTH TO WEYMOUTH

COUNTRY RAILWAY ROUTES
BATH TO EVERCREECH JUNCTION
BOURNEMOUTH TO EVERCREECH JUNCTION
READING TO GUILDFORD
WOKING TO ALTON

SOUTHERN MAIN LINES
WOKING TO PORTSMOUTH
HAYWARDS HEATH TO SEAFORD
EPSOM TO HORSHAM
CRAWLEY TO LITTLEHAMPTON
THREE BRIDGES TO BRIGHTON
WATERLOO TO WOKING
VICTORIA TO EAST CROYDON
TONBRIDGE TO HASTINGS
EAST CROYDON TO THREE BRIDGES
WOKING TO SOUTHAMPTON
WATERLOO TO WINDSOR
LONDON BRIDGE TO EAST CROYDON

STEAMING THROUGH
STEAMING THROUGH KENT
STEAMING THROUGH EAST HANTS
STEAMING THROUGH EAST SUSSEX
STEAMING THROUGH SURREY
STEAMING THROUGH WEST SUSSEX
STEAMING THROUGH THE
  ISLE OF WIGHT

OTHER RAILWAY BOOKS
WAR ON THE LINE
(Reprint of the SR history in World War II)
GARRAWAY FATHER AND SON
(Biography - includes LNER, Talyllyn and Festiniog Railways)
INDUSTRIAL RAILWAYS OF THE SOUTH-EAST

OTHER BOOKS
MIDHURST TOWN – THEN & NOW
EAST GRINSTEAD – THEN & NOW
THE MILITARY DEFENCE OF WEST SUSSEX
WEST SUSSEX WATERWAYS
SURREY WATERWAYS
BATTLE OVER PORTSMOUTH
A City at war in 1940
SUSSEX POLICE FORCES

*Video also available. Details from
M.P. Videos, 11 Park Crescent, Midhurst,
West Sussex GU29 9ED.*